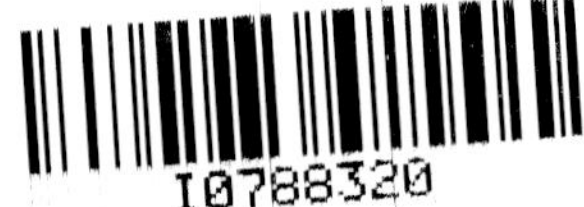

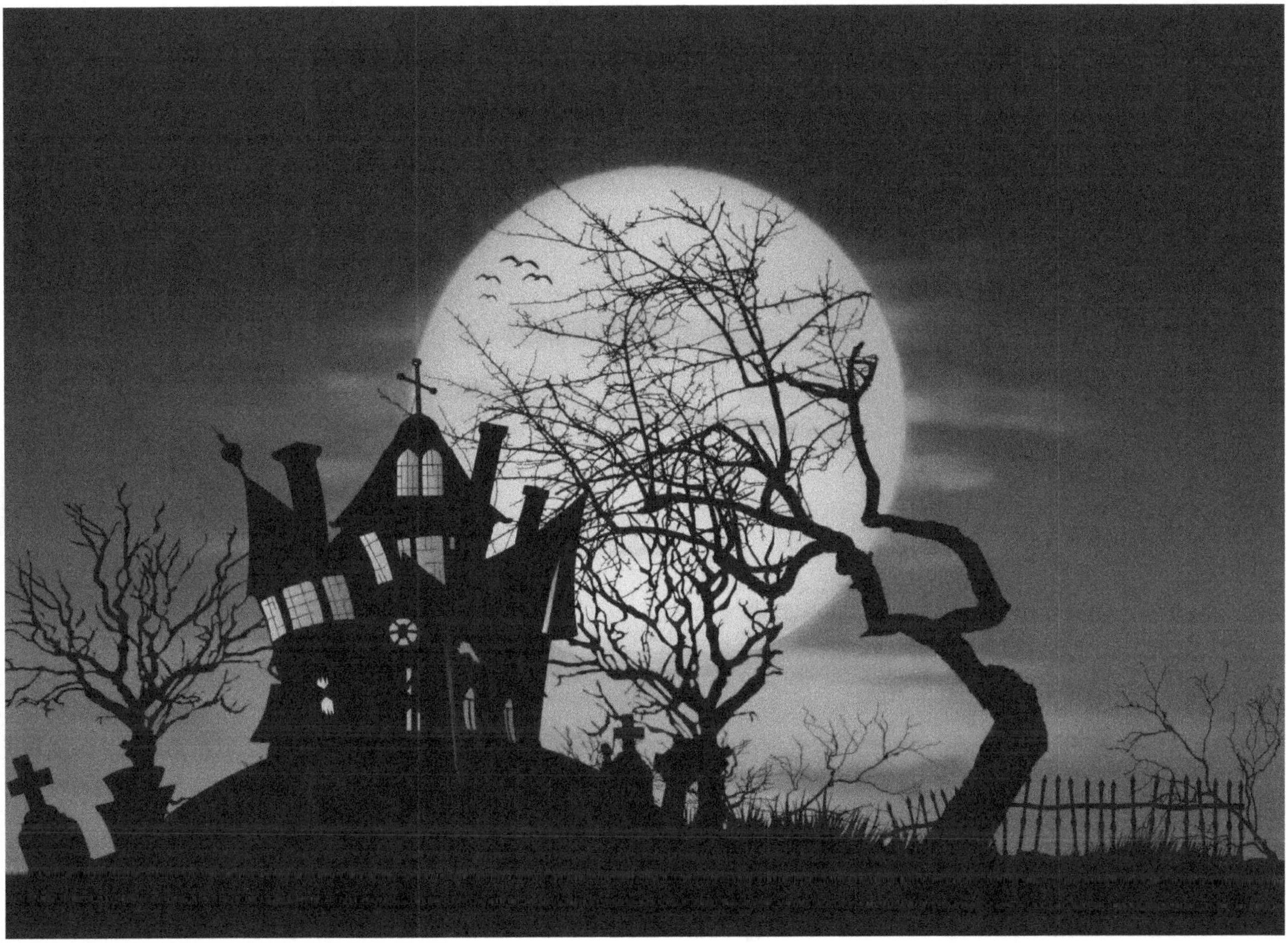

JUMBO HALLOWEEN COLORING BOOK FOR KIDS AGES 2-5

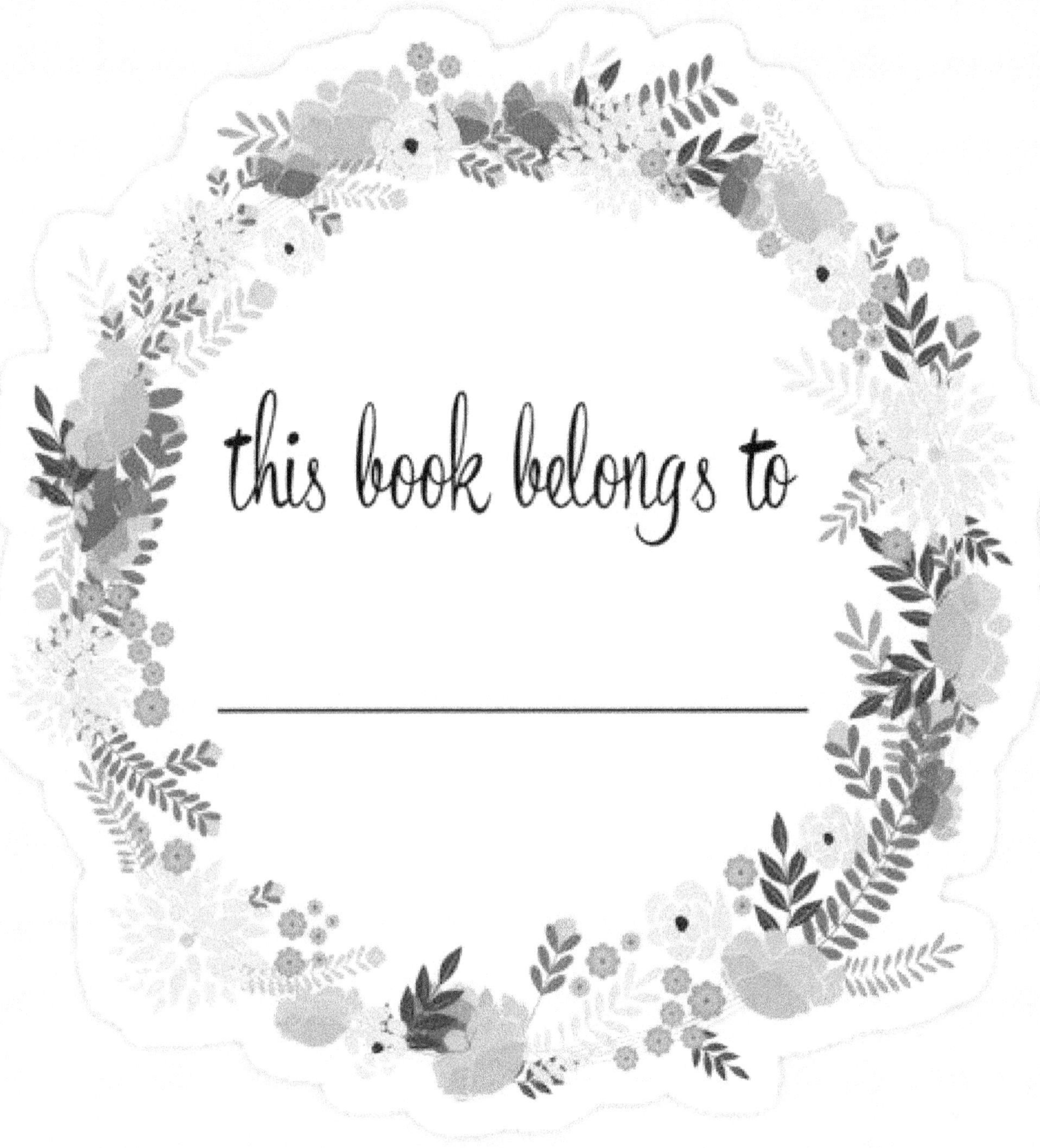
this book belongs to

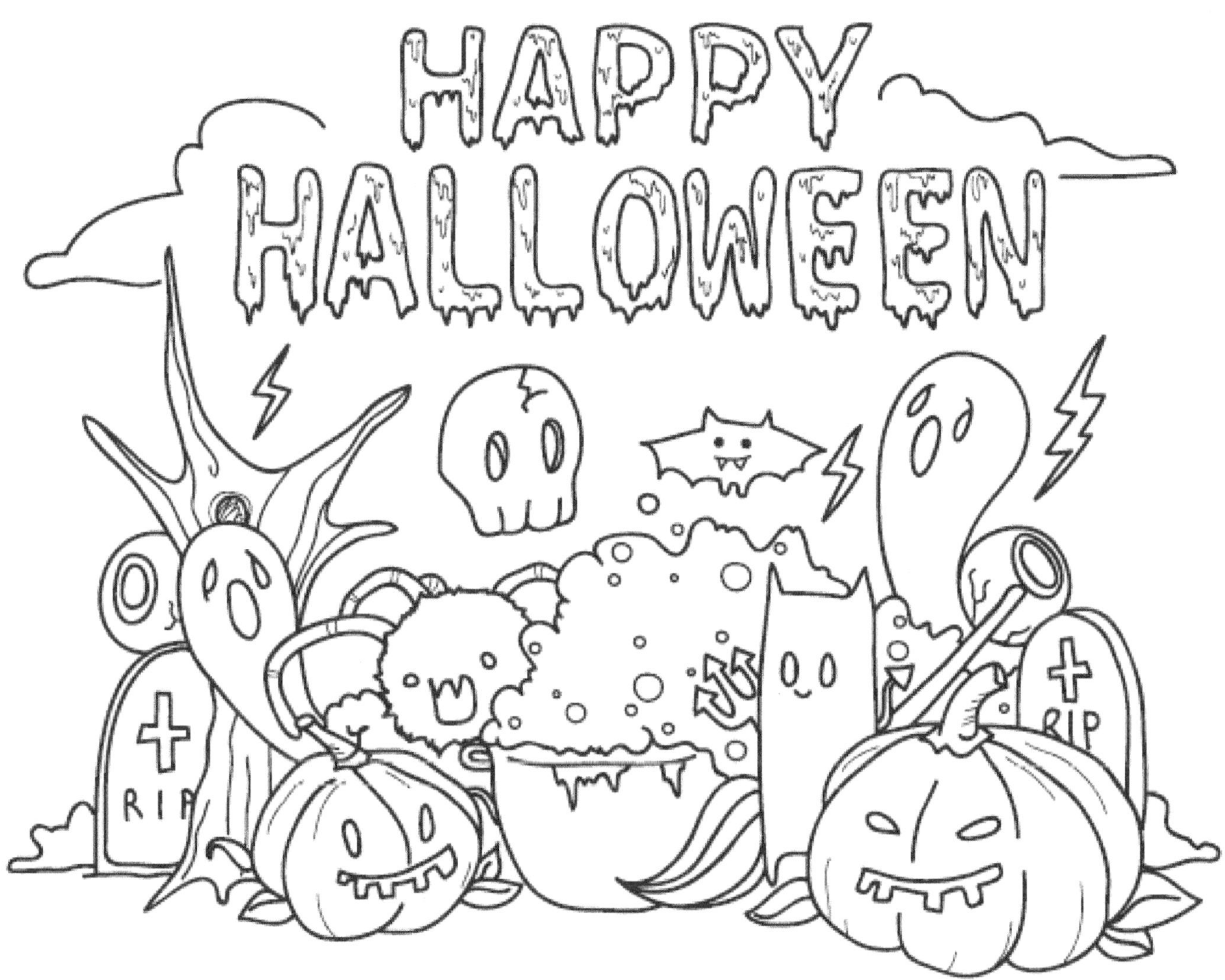

HAPPY HALLOWEEN
RIP
RIP

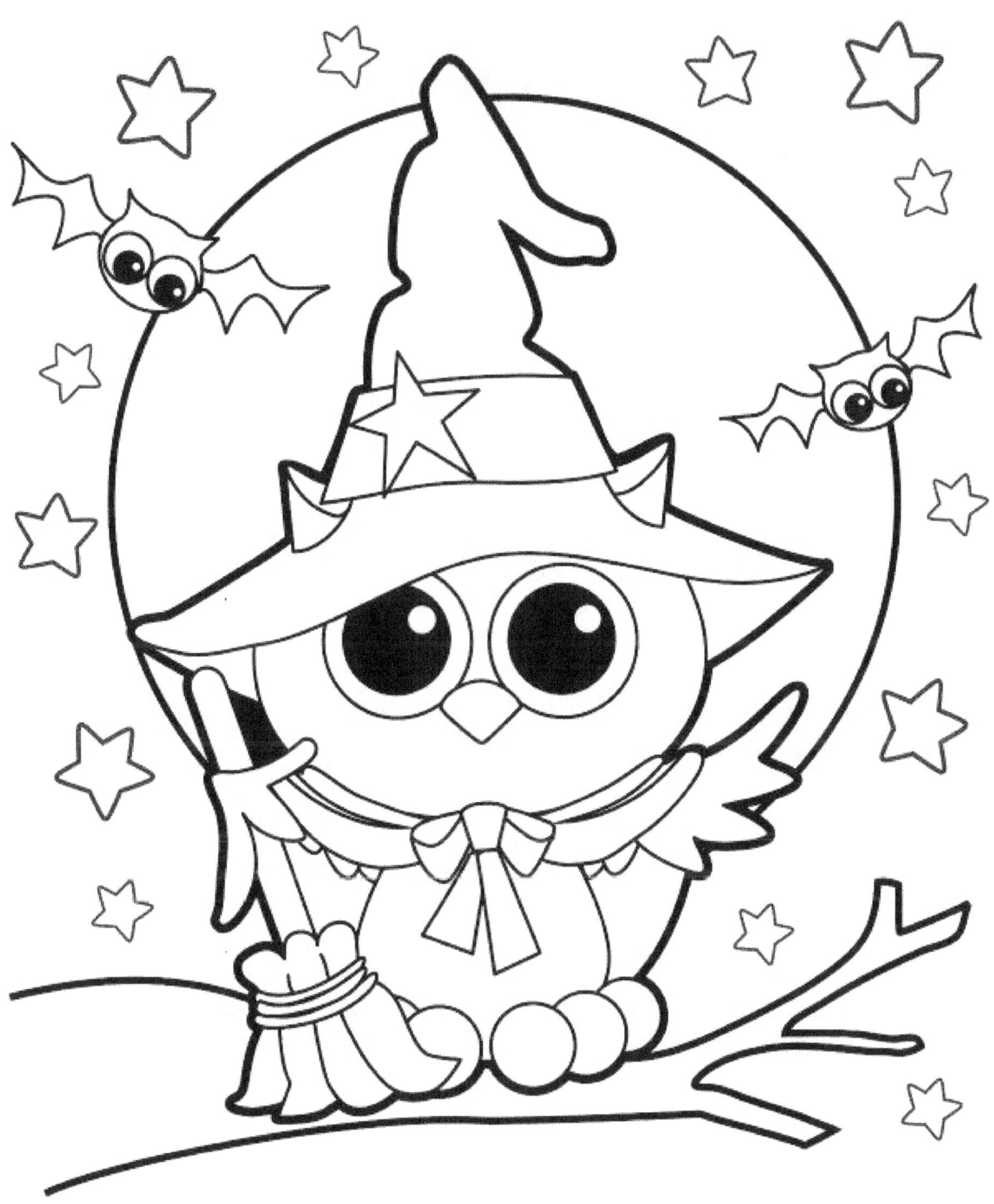

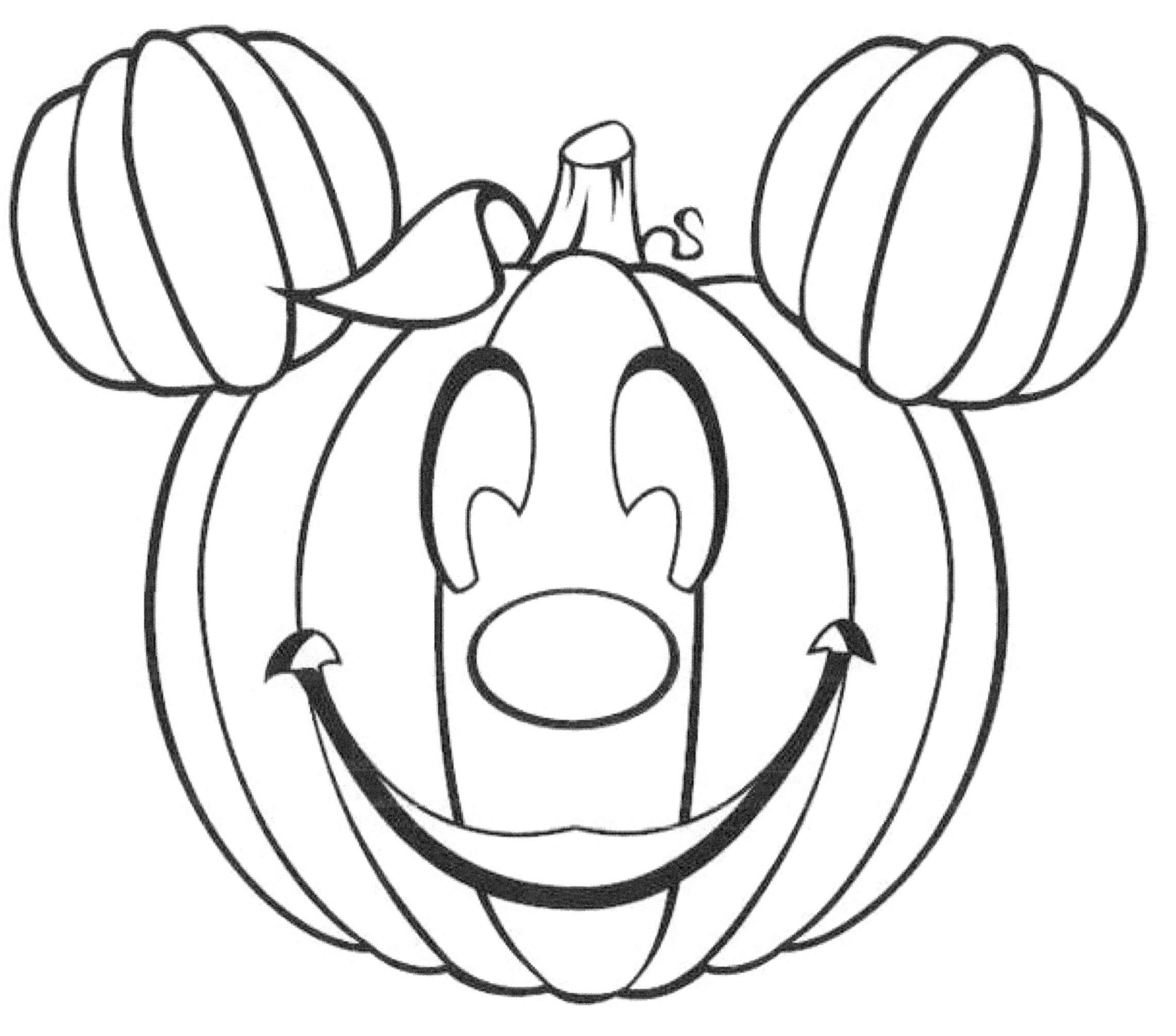

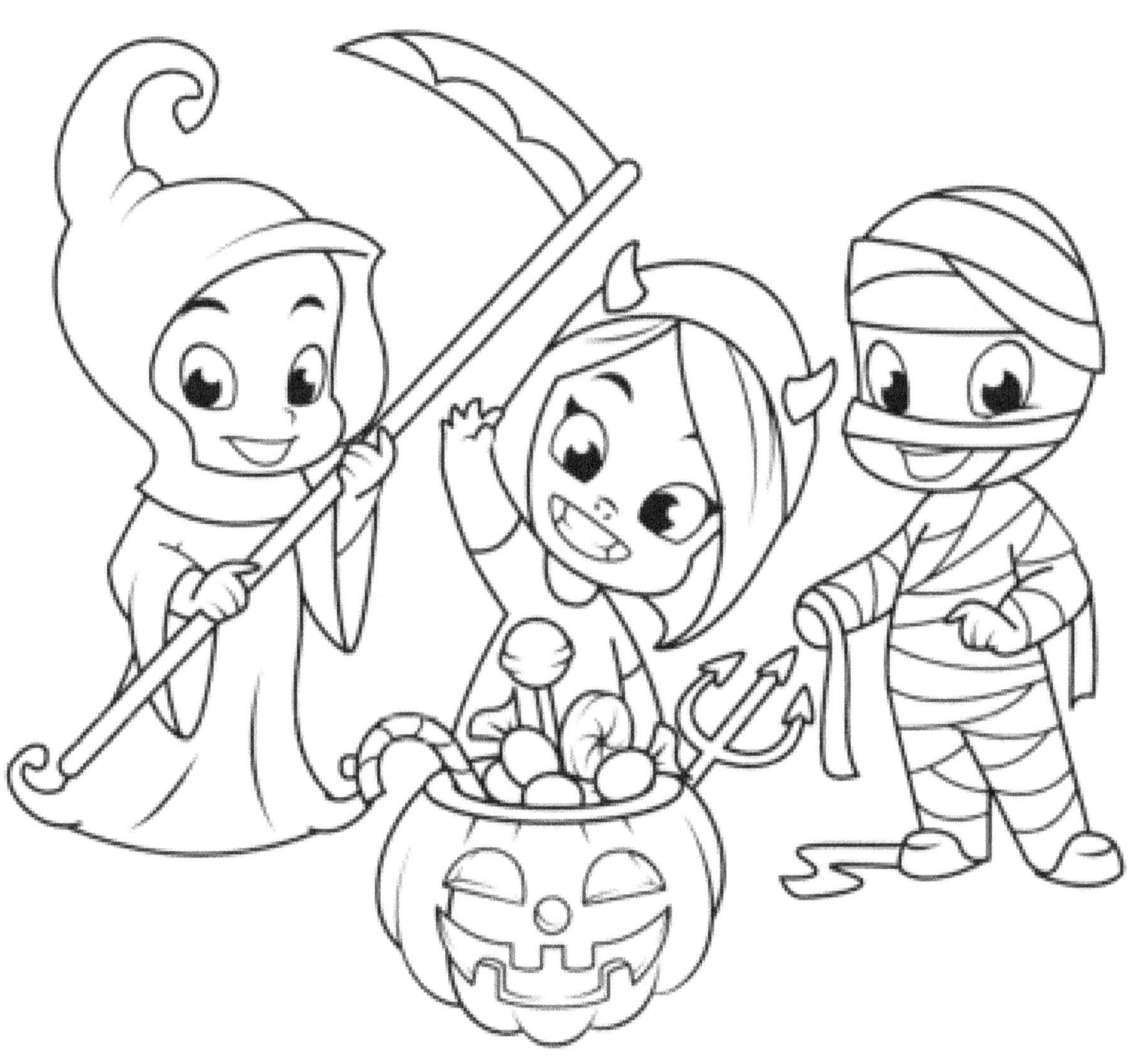

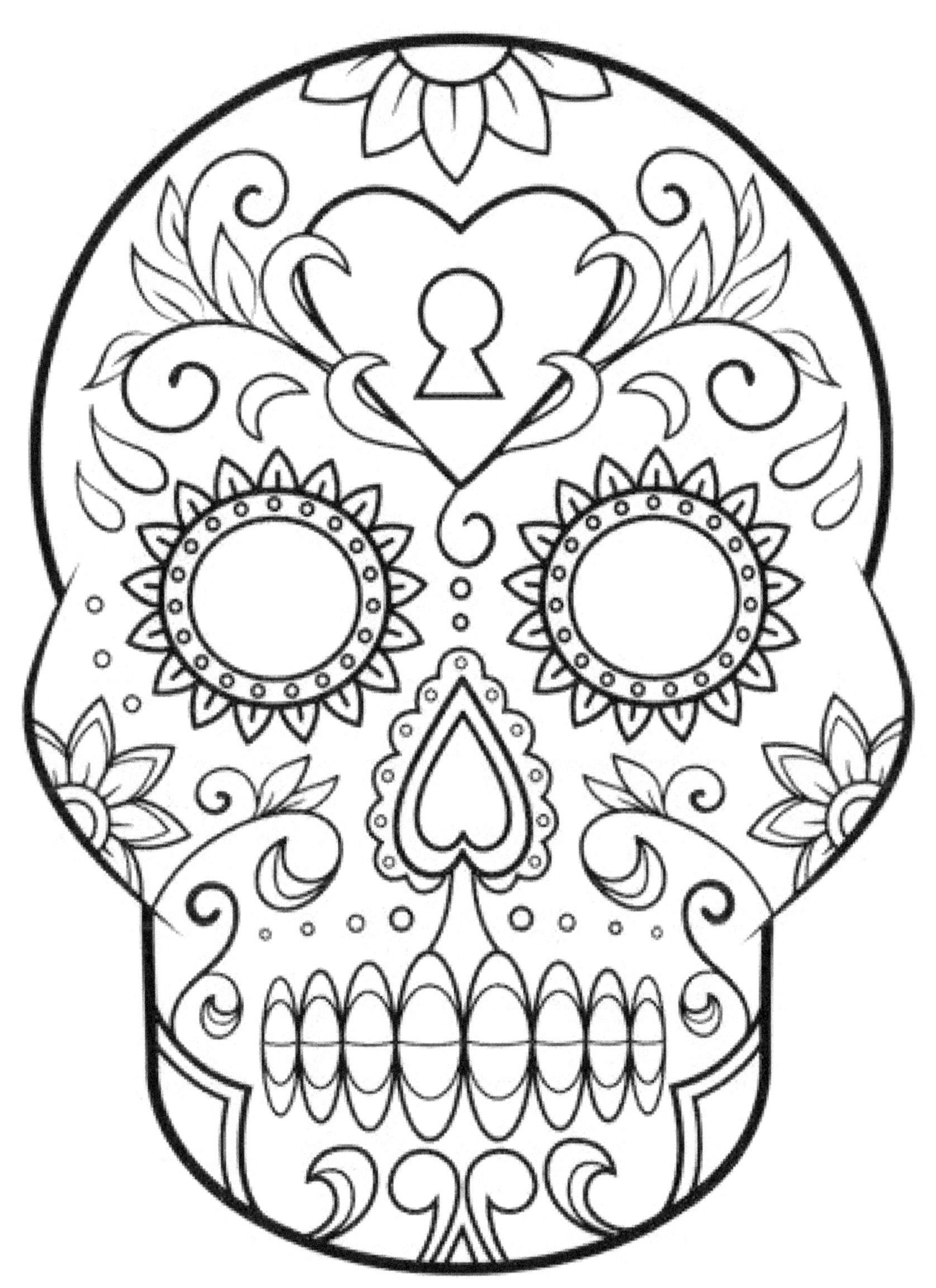

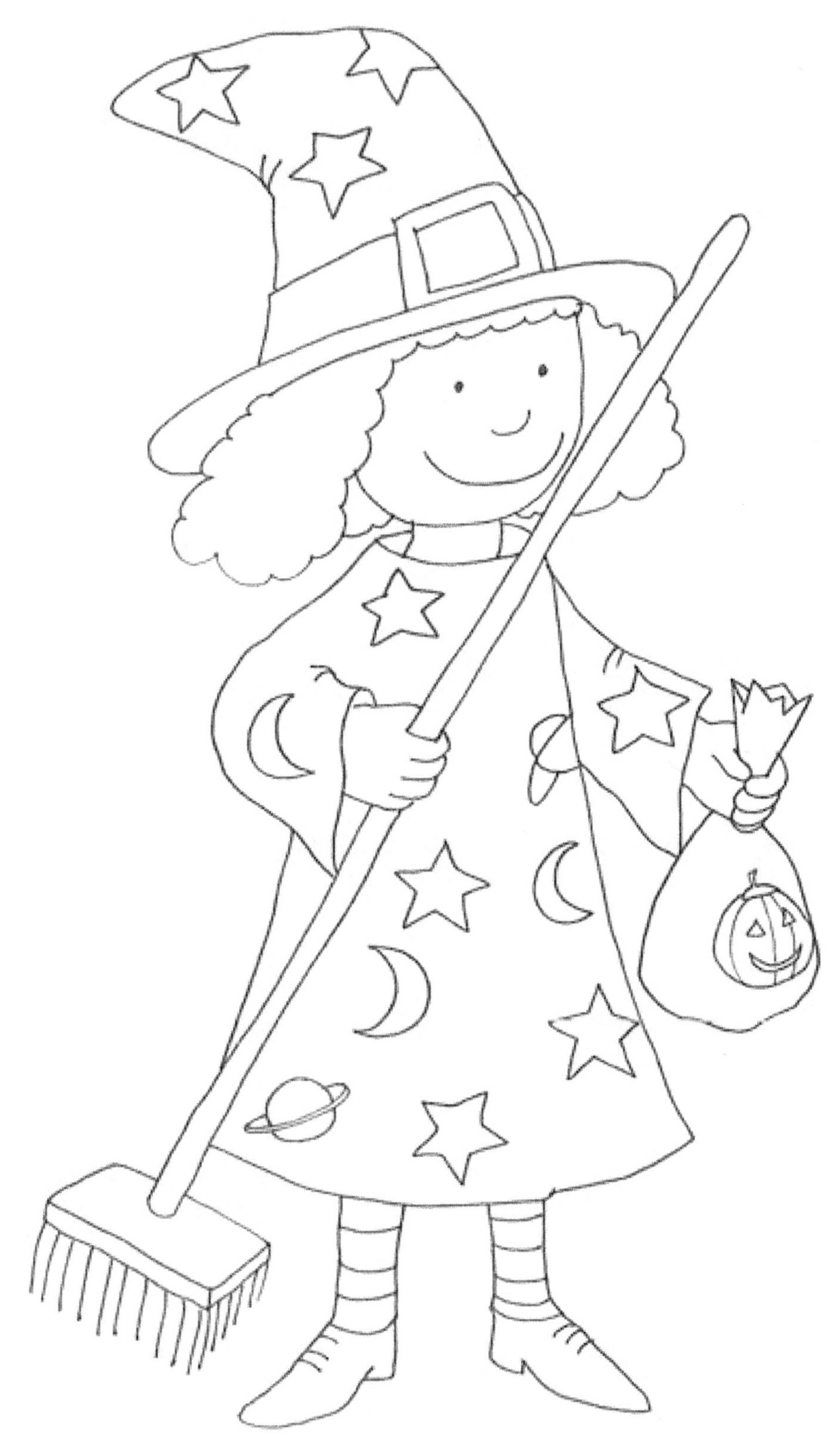

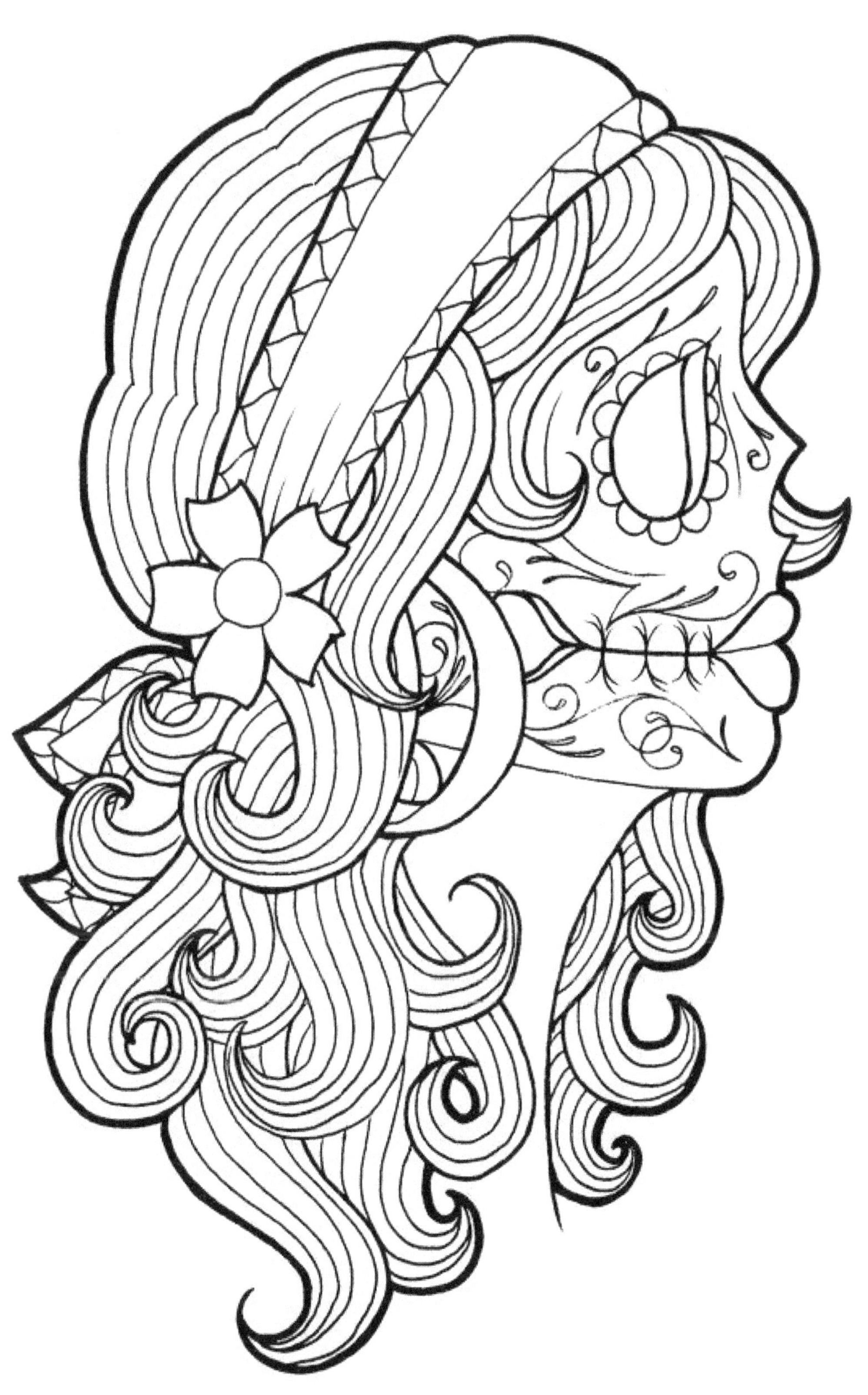

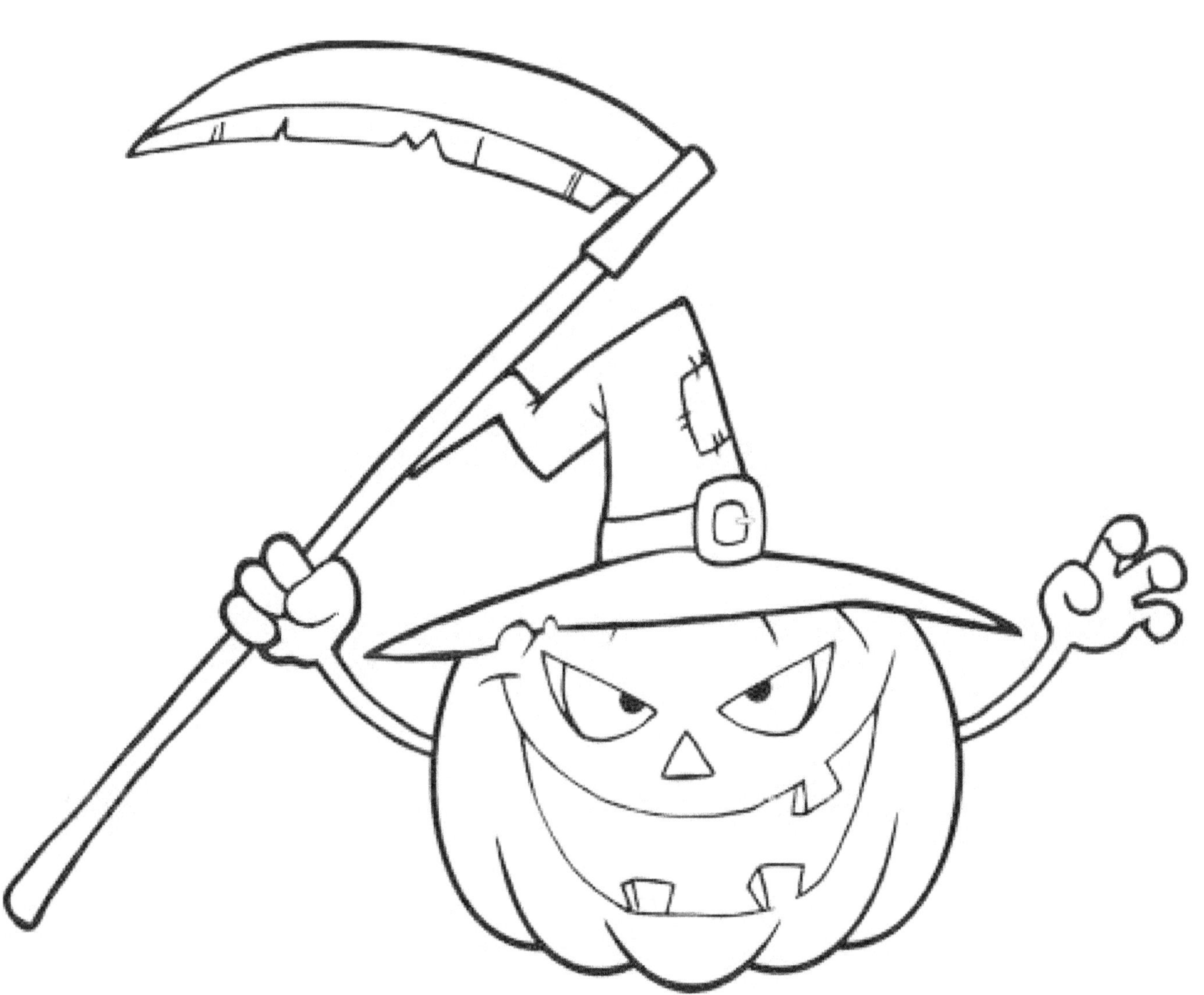

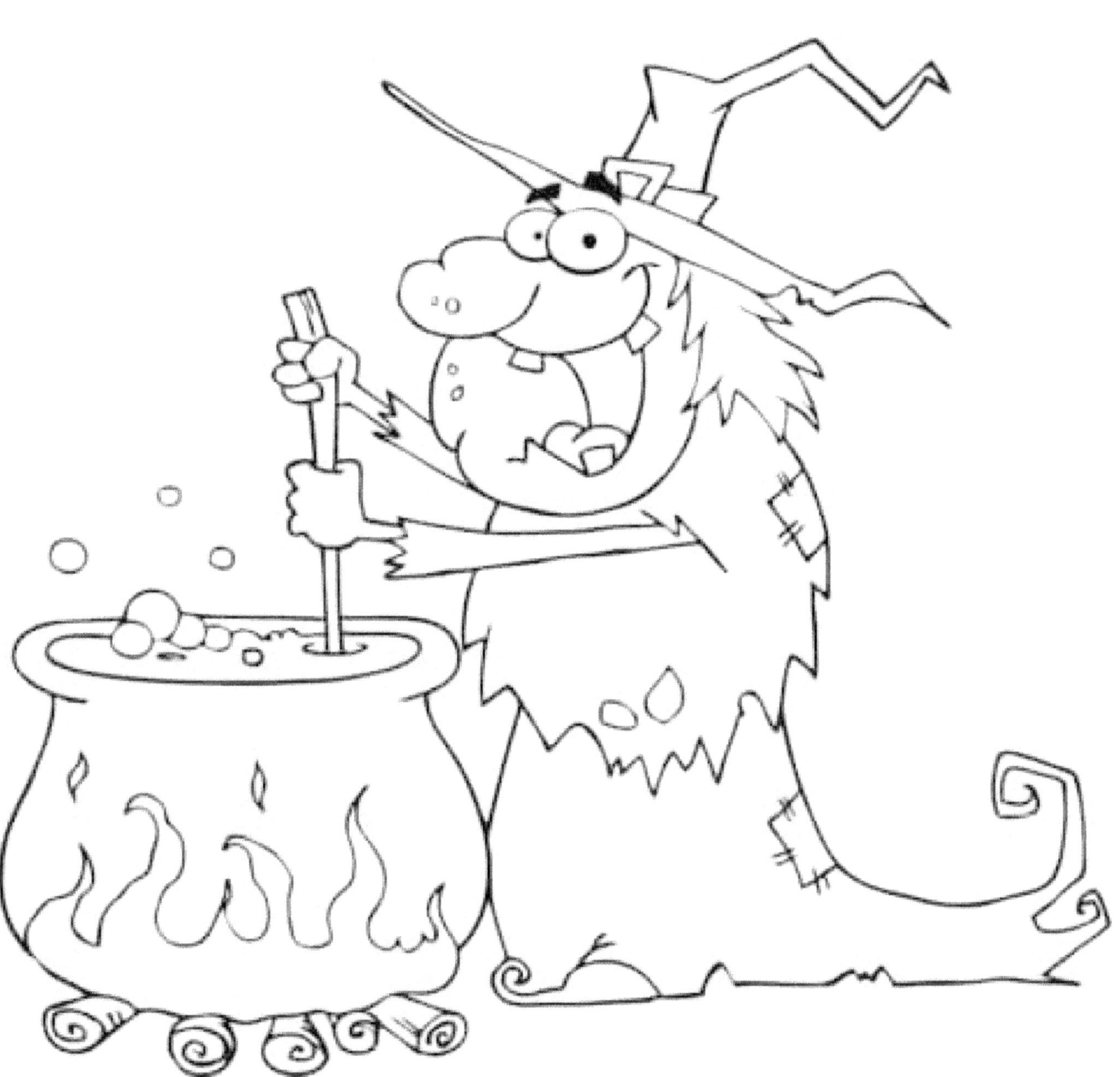

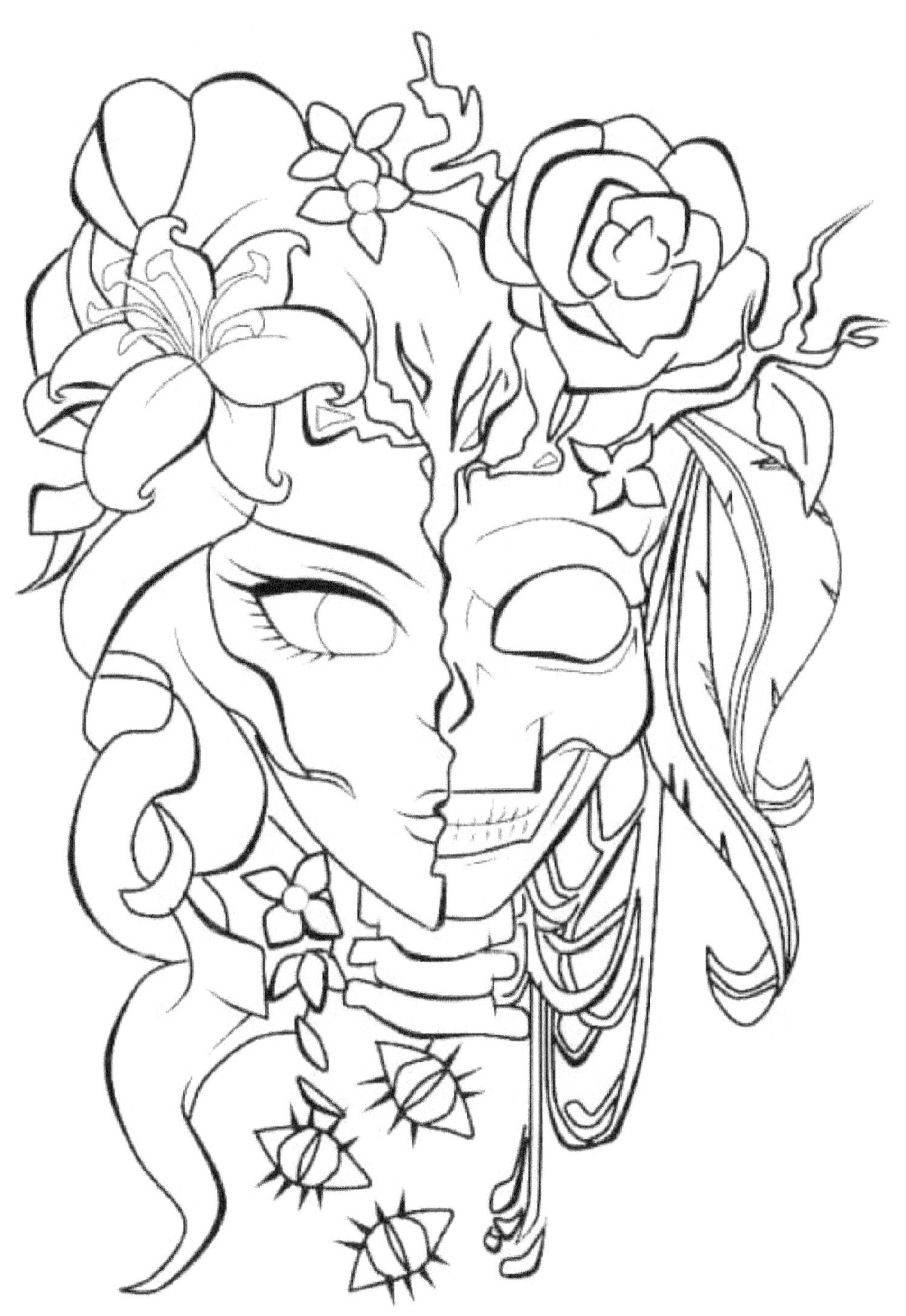

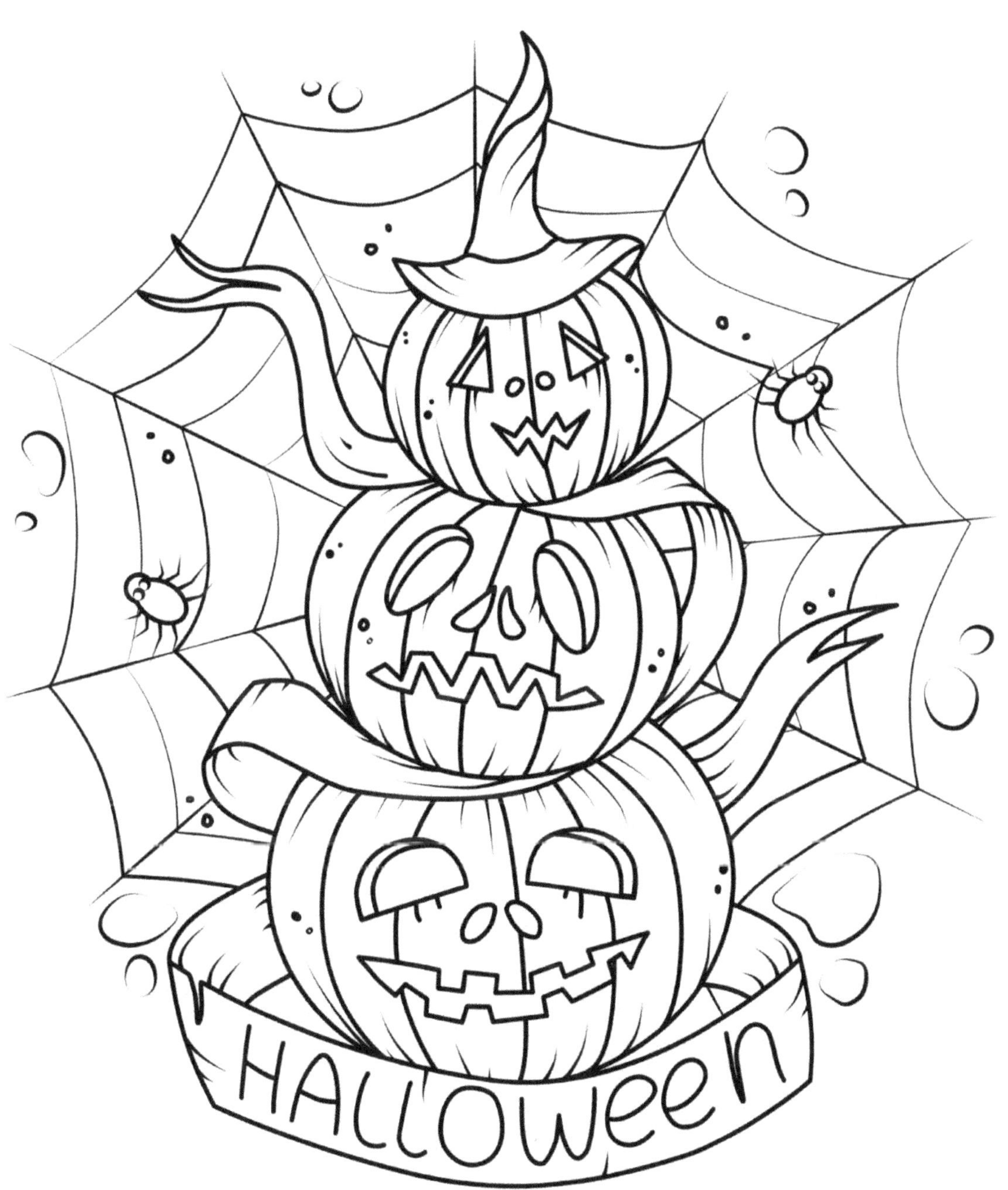
HALLOWEEN

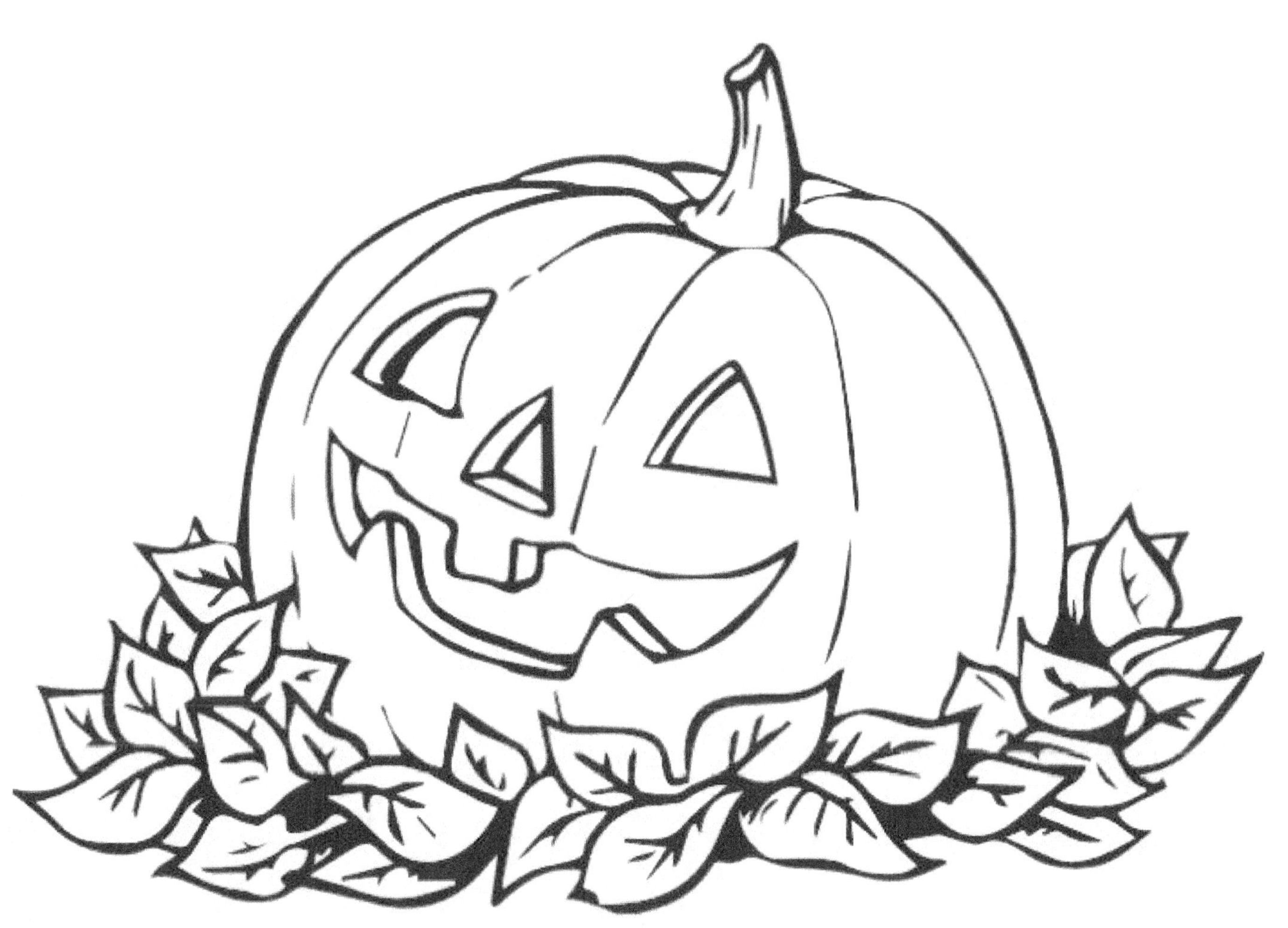

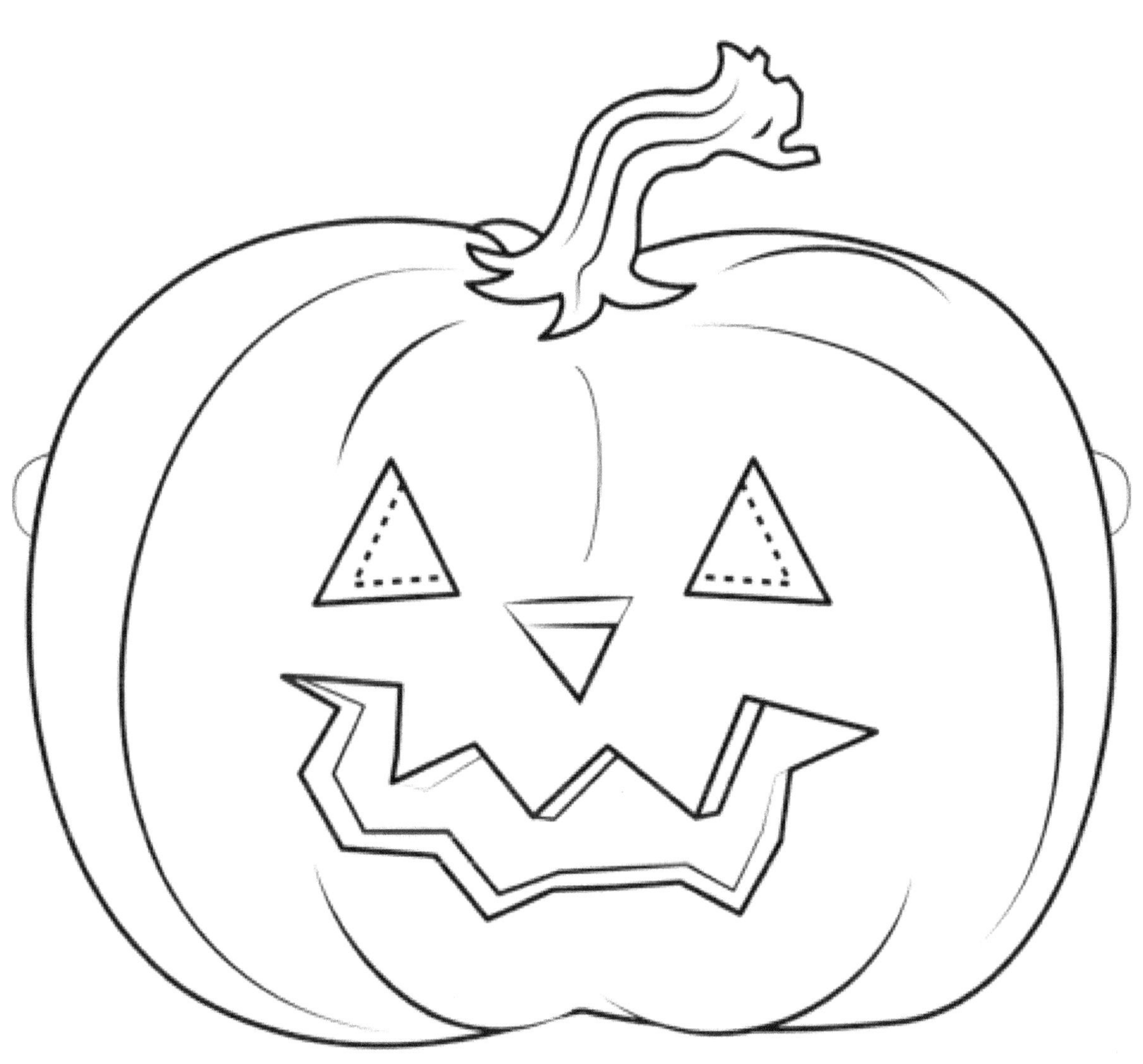

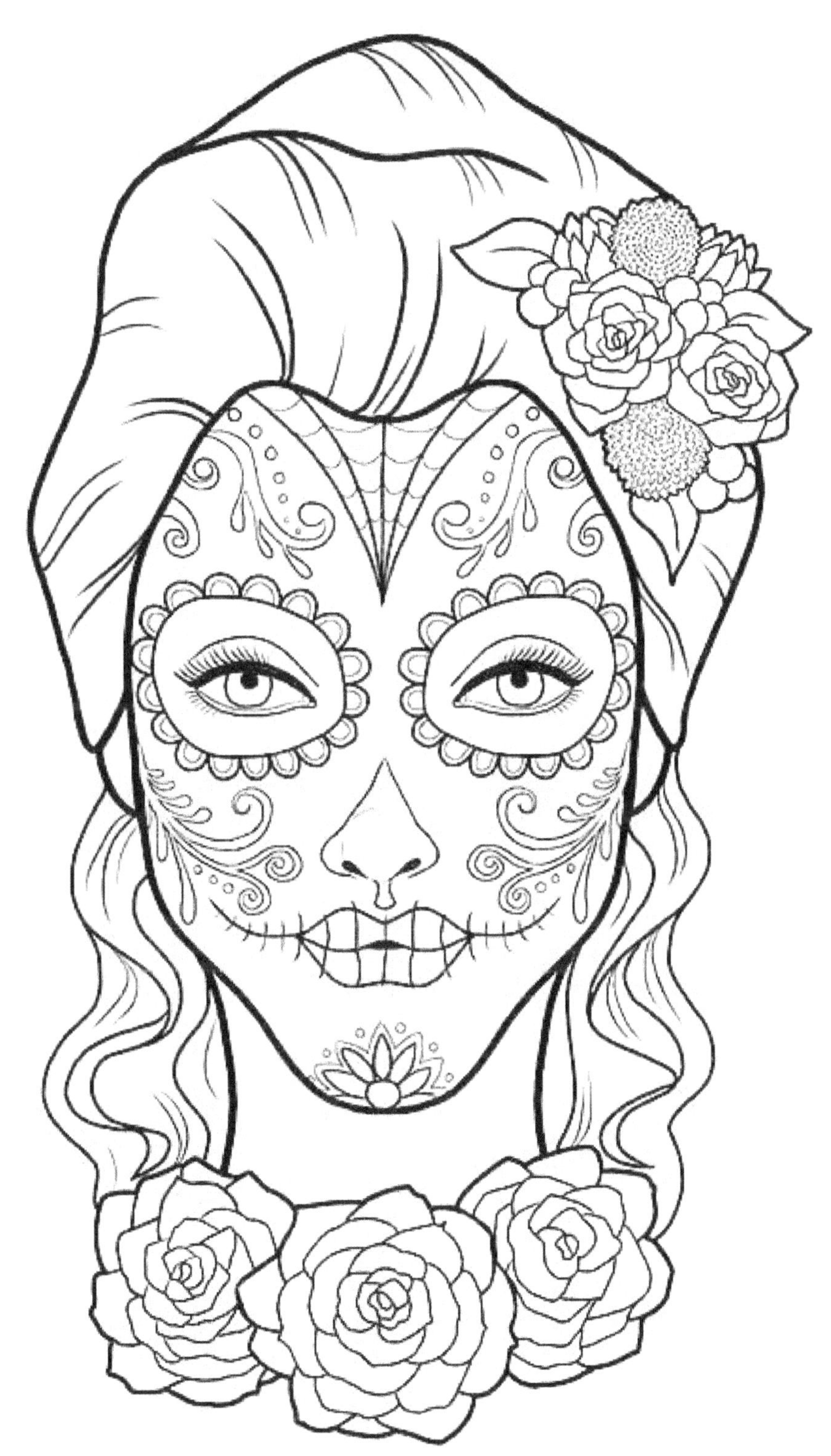

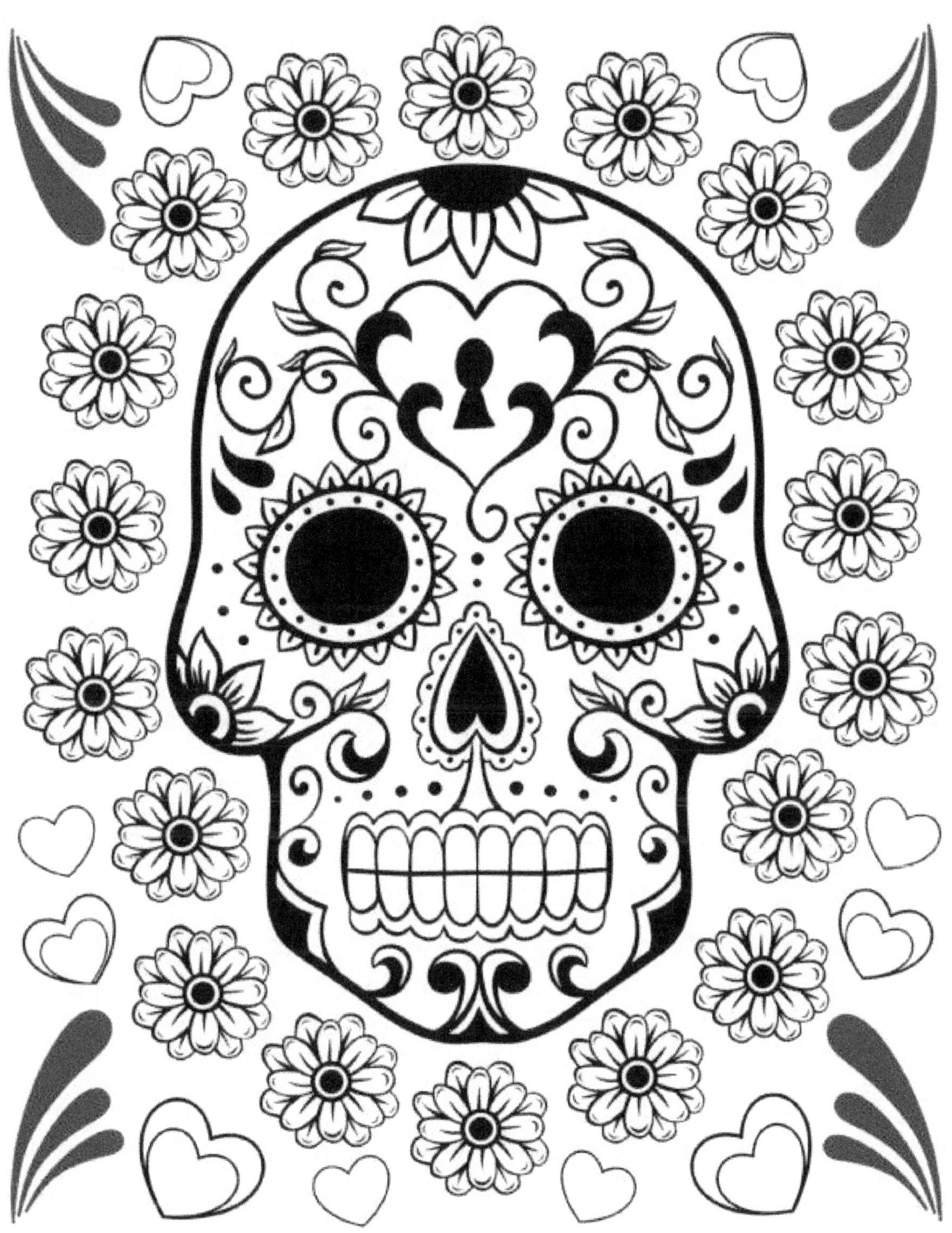

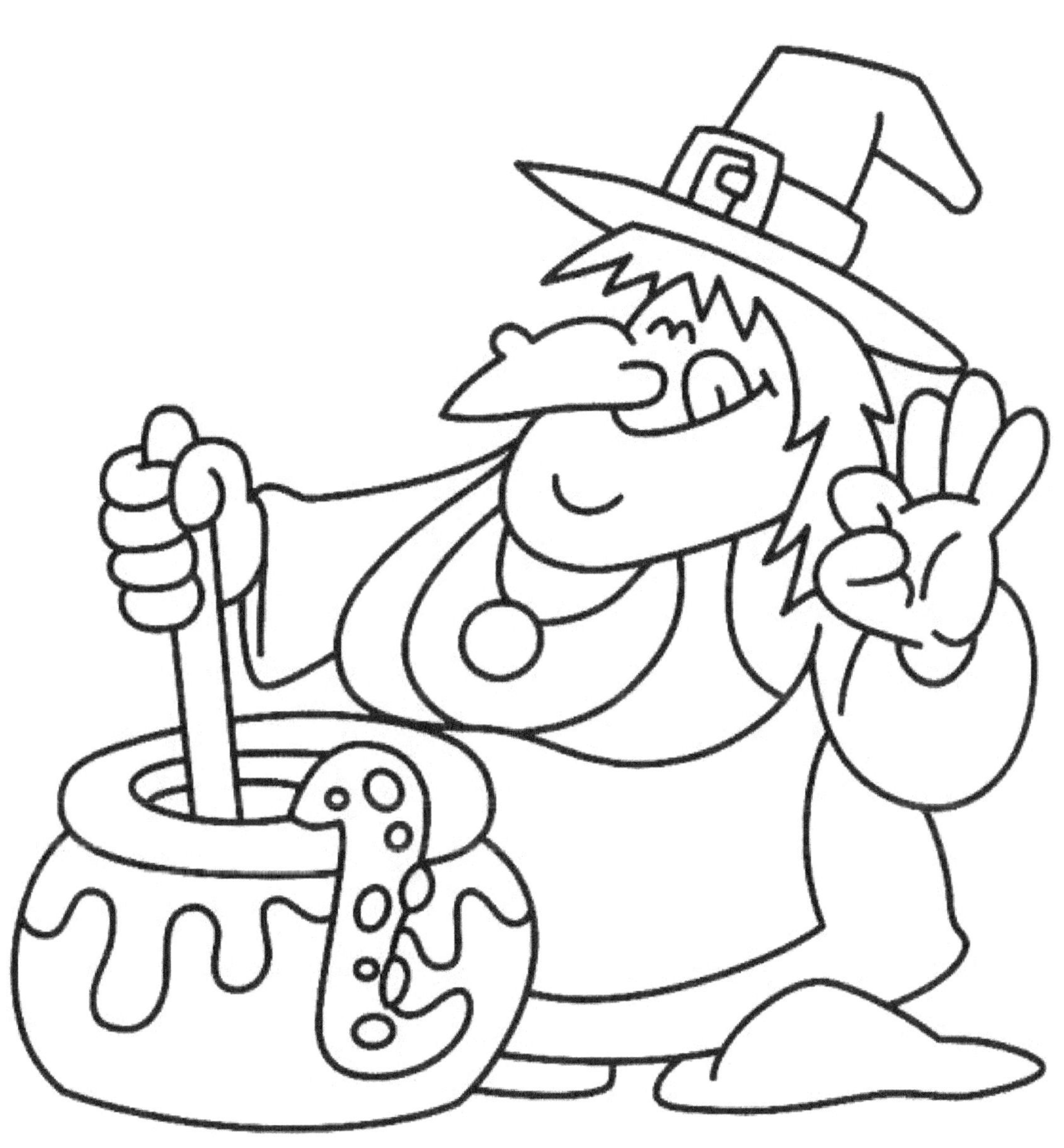

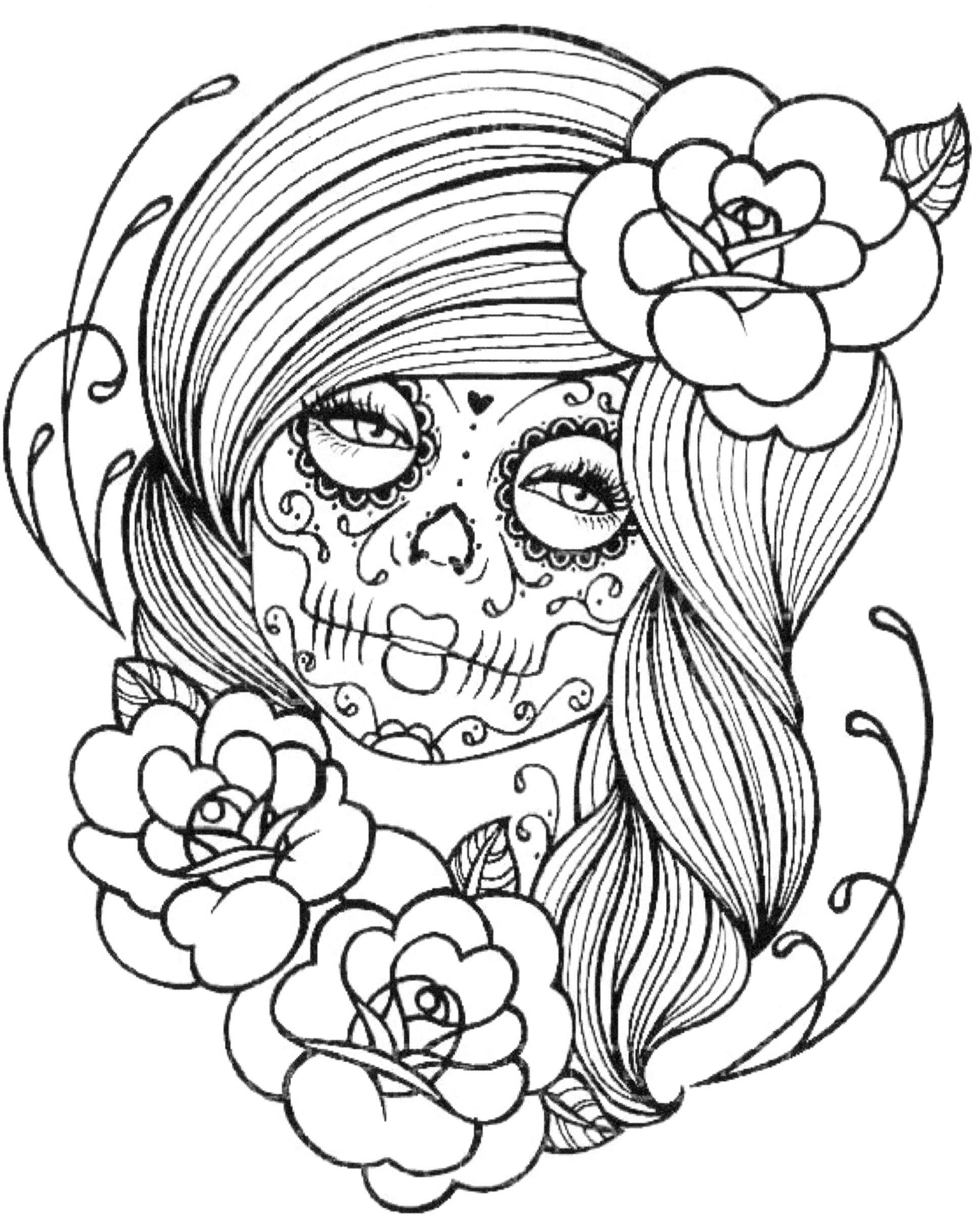

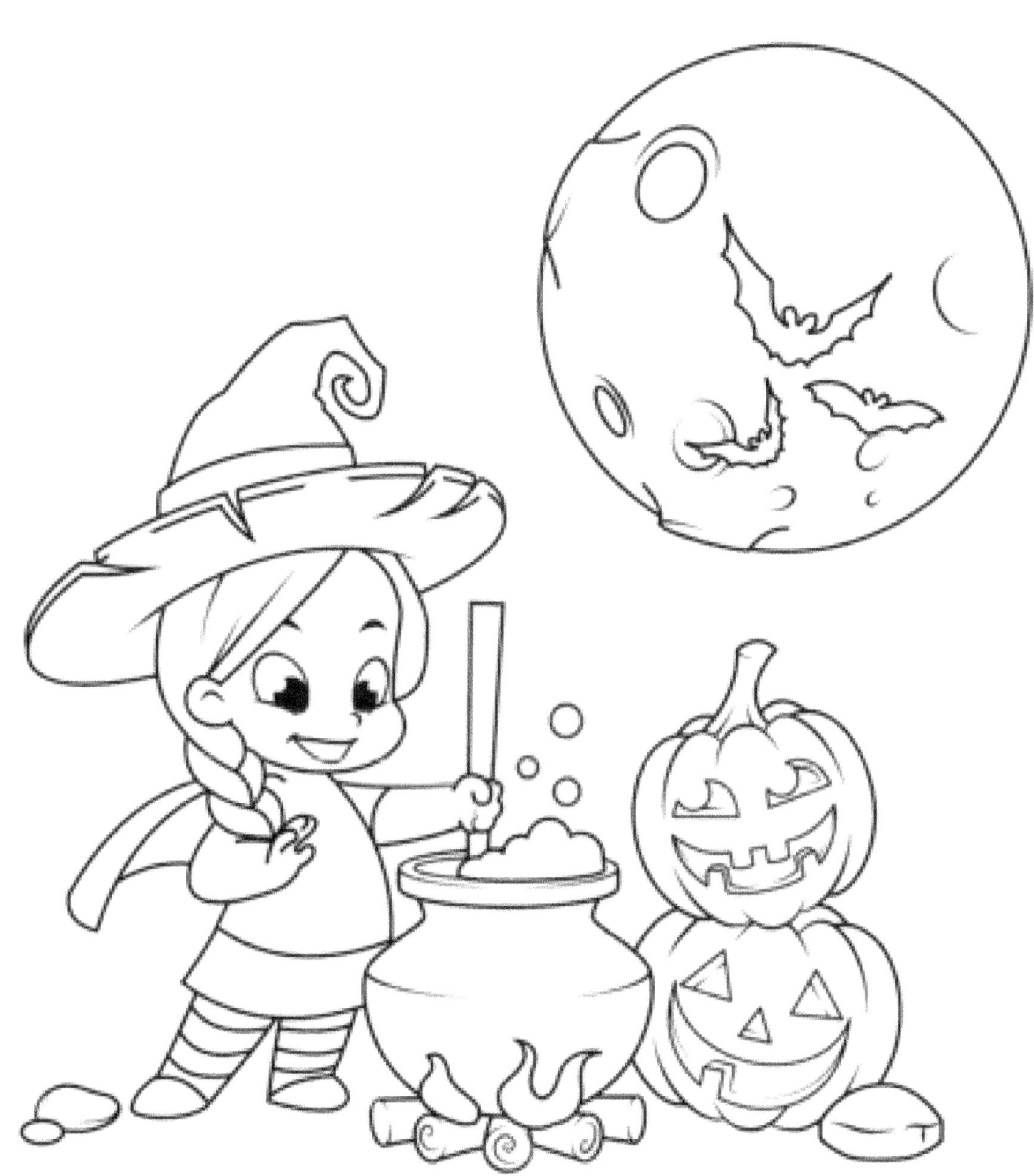

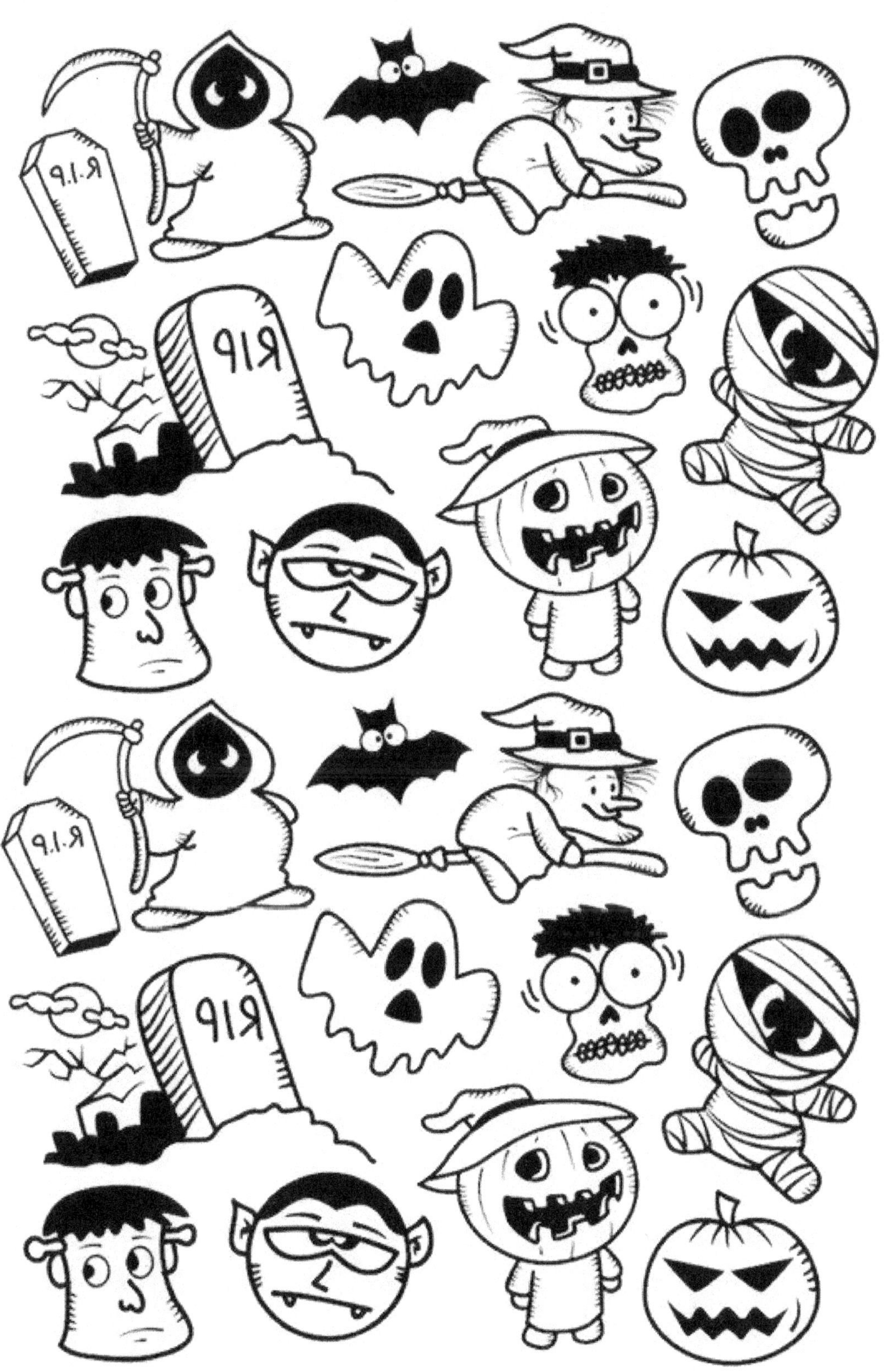

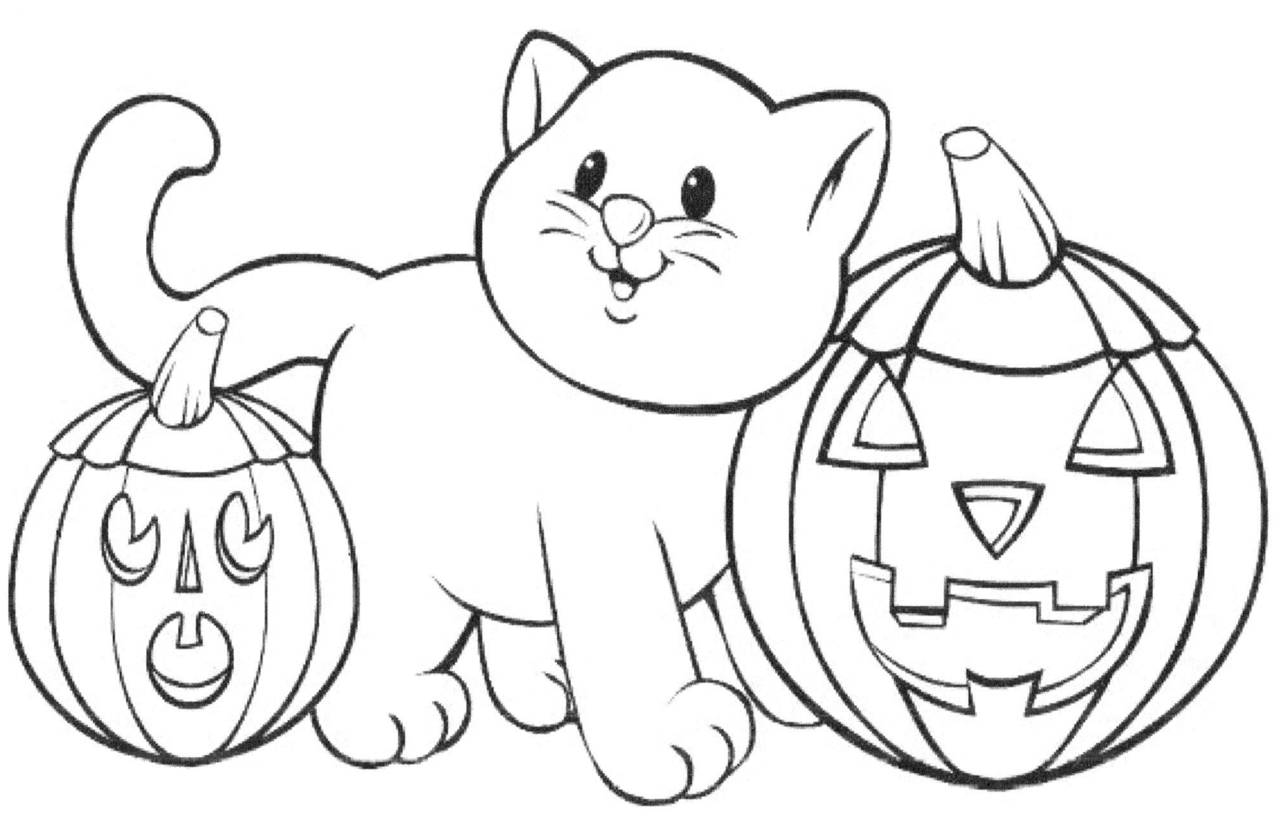

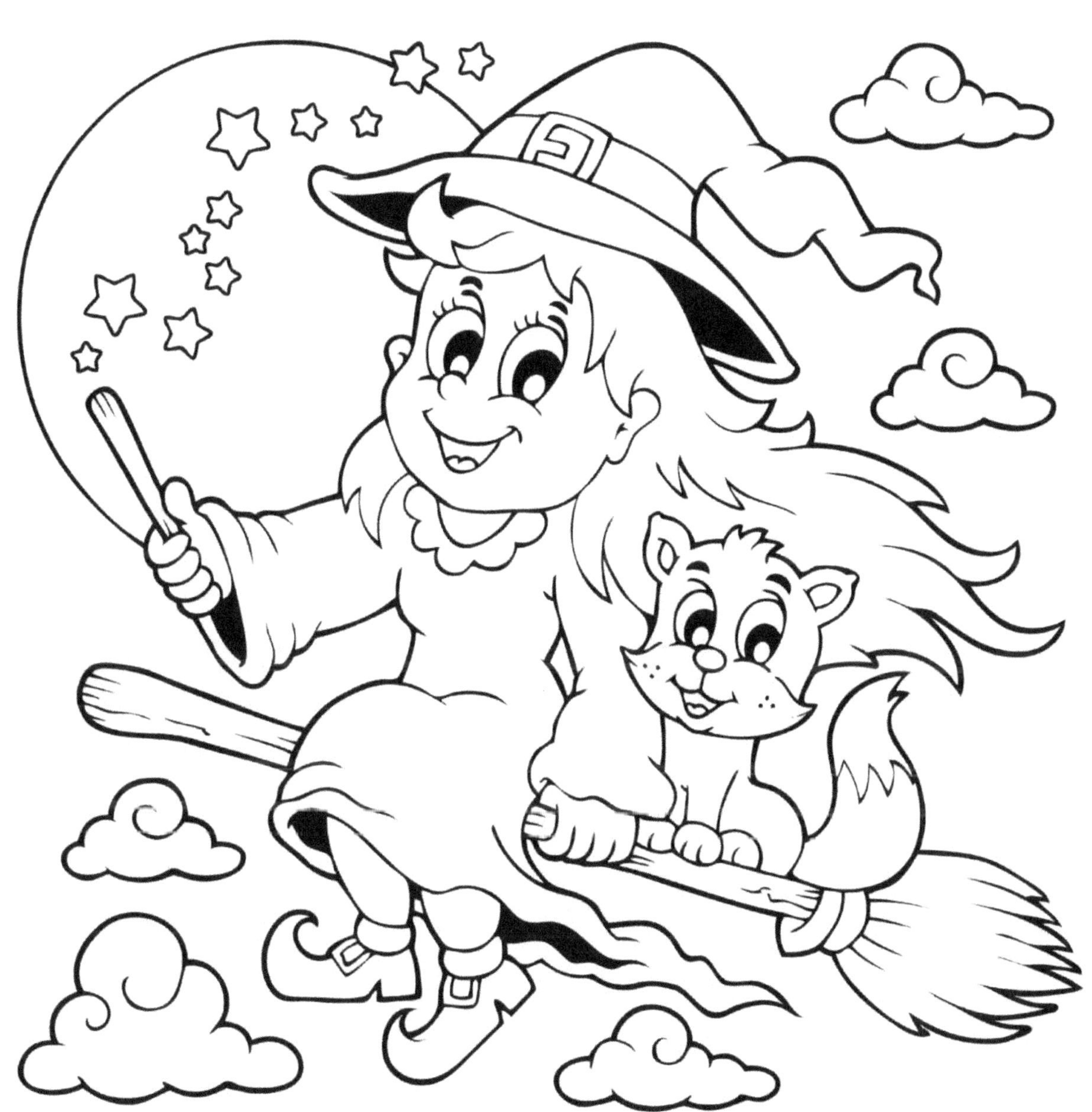

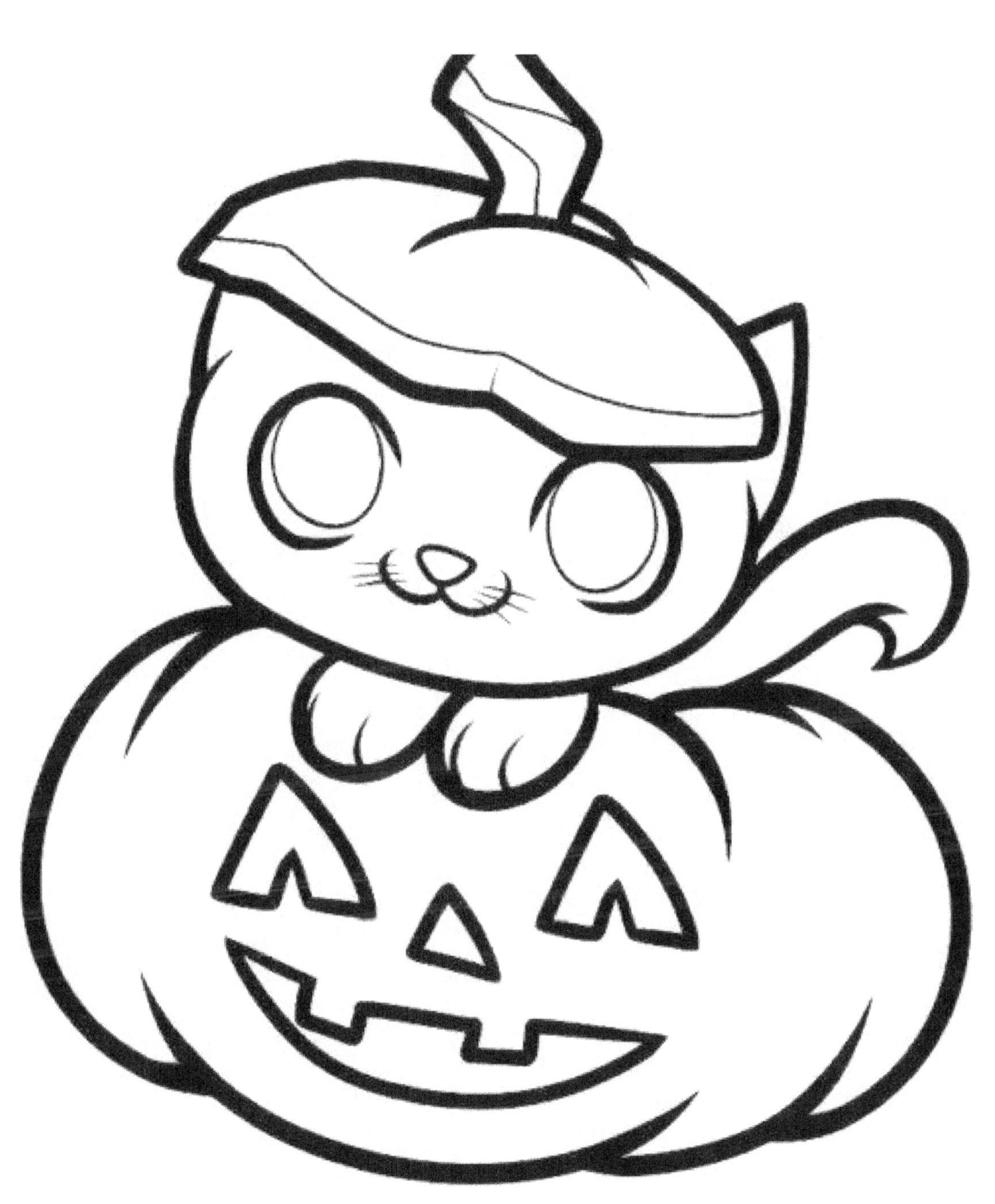

TANK YOU